V&A
Foolscap Editions

British Mosques

Edited by
Shahed Saleem
Christopher Turner
Ella Kilgallon

Foreword
Tristram Hunt
13

Introduction
Christopher Turner
15

The Ramadan Pavilion
Christopher Turner
Shahed Saleem
23

Documenting the mosque in the V&A Collections
Ella Kilgallon
45

Tracing the elements of the British mosque
Shahed Saleem
55

Three British Mosques
Shahed Saleem
Christopher Turner
Ella Kilgallon
85

Assembly: performing the materiality of Muslim prayer space
Julie Marsh
113

Acknowledgements
127

Biographies
131

Foreword
Tristram Hunt, Director of the Victoria and Albert Museum

British Mosques represents the culmination of a collaborative research initiative by Shahed Saleem and Julie Marsh of the University of Westminster, and Christopher Turner and Ella Kilgallon, curators at the Victoria and Albert Museum. Building on Saleem's foundational study of the British mosque (published in 2018), two major projects curated by the V&A's Department for Design, Architecture and Digital explore the architecture of the mosque in Britain.

The V&A is home to one of the world's largest collections of Islamic art from the Middle East and has collected art from the Islamic world since it was founded in 1857. This impressive collection, the highlights of which are on display in the Jameel Gallery, continues to influence architects and designers. The Ramadan Pavilion, an installation at the V&A designed by Saleem with architecture students at the University of Westminster, takes inspiration from the V&A's Islamic collections as well as the history of the British mosque. A collage of Islamic architectural elements, the pavilion creates a visual commentary on the Orientalist representation of Islam and the lived experience of British Muslims.

The second edition of the International Architecture Exhibition – La Biennale di Venezia (1982-83) presented an overview of architecture in Islamic countries. For the Biennale Architettura 2021, the V&A presents *Three British Mosques* in the Pavilion of Applied Arts, an exploration of the creative and complex cultural exchanges that enrich our urban landscape. Responding to curator Hashim Sarkis's theme, *How will we live together?*, Saleem, Turner and Kilgallon explore contemporary multiculturalism through three mosques in London adapted from existing buildings. As mosques such as these evolve and, in many cases, are demolished and rebuilt, the V&A is documenting and celebrating a crucial phase in the journey of Muslim architecture before it is lost.

The V&A is the world's most comprehensive architectural resource – home to monumental plaster casts, large-scale architectural fragments and entire historic rooms, as well as models, drawings and sketchbooks. With this programme in London and Venice, the Department for Design, Architecture and Digital continues to explore new modes of collection, curation and public engagement. Digital 3D scans of the three London mosques and test pieces from the Brick Lane Mosque minaret will now become valued additions to the museum's national collection of architecture.

Introduction

Christopher Turner

The Mosque, Woking

Introduction
Christopher Turner

In 2002, architecture critic Jonathan Glancey asked in *The Guardian*: 'Why are there no great British mosques?' He praised the first purpose-built mosque in Britain, constructed in Woking in 1889 by W.L. Chambers, as a 'delightful Moghul, or Indo-Saracenic, pavilion'. With its green onion dome and minarets, the mock-Oriental structure was a site of high culture, where the *Islamic Review* was published and the first English translation of the Qur'an produced; where the idea of a Muslim state separate from India was debated, and the name for it, Pakistan, first coined. Glancey considered all of the mosques built since to be 'run-of-the-mill', 'determinedly glum ... brick boxes with minarets and domes applied like afterthoughts'. He attributed this to the mass migration of the 1960s and 70s from newly independent, post-colonial countries to fulfil demands for cheap labour in Britain, and determined that the resulting poverty was at the root of the UK's 'poor mosque design'.

In *The British Mosque: An Architectural and Social History* (2018), Shahed Saleem – the architect of striking contemporary UK mosques, including one in Bethnal Green with a facade inspired by the pattern of an Iranian tile on display in the Victoria and Albert Museum's Jameel Gallery – suggests a more nuanced, generous, anthropological view. Rather than interpreting and dismissing neo-traditionalist mosques as kitsch pastiche – the crude importation of a pre-existing Muslim culture from another place – he prefers to look at mosque-making as a creative, performative process by which immigrant communities construct their identities anew in foreign cities. 'The replication and reuse of Islamic architectural symbols from history,' he writes, 'rather than being the ill-considered application of the past, is instead a statement of where that group sees itself, and its relation to the wider world, and is part of the process of becoming for minority communities.'

The first mosque structure in Britain was an eighteenth-century folly built by William Chambers at Kew Gardens. Based on Turkish Islamic architecture and flanked by two minarets, it was one of several temples and garden buildings constructed at the time, of which only the Chinese Pagoda remains. Saleem will revisit this folly in a brightly coloured Ramadan Pavilion to be installed in the V&A's Sackler Courtyard in spring 2022. Designed for Ramadan and the London Festival of Architecture, for which the museum is the cultural hub, it riffs off the domes and arches of the V&A's architecture as well as the mosque elements on display in the Islamic galleries. In collaboration with the Ramadan Tent Project, the pavilion will provide a venue for 'Open Iftar', bringing together communities after sunset for conversations and to break the fast. 'The Ramadan Pavilion is the counterpoint to the Kew folly as it represents Muslim life and culture in Britain, rather than a symbol of something distant and exotic,' Saleem explains. He deliberately intended to confront the power struc-

A hand-coloured postcard of the Shah Jahan Mosque in Woking, the first built in Britain in 1889 tures of Orientalism by 'taking ownership of one's image and creating architecture from that, and placing it within a significant cultural institution born in the colonial period'.

The British mosque is also the subject of the V&A's contribution to the 17th International Architecture Exhibition – La Biennale di Venezia 2021, directed by the Lebanese architect Hakim Sarkis (designer of a mosque in Doha) under the theme, *How will we live together?*. The 'we' of the title begs the question: to which 'we' do we refer? Saleem has co-curated (with V&A curators Ella Kilgallon and the author) an exhibition in the Pavilion of Applied Arts – a Special Project between the V&A and La Biennale di Venezia – that explores themes of immigration, hybridity and multiculturalism through a study of three London mosques and their communities: Brick Lane Mosque, known for its High Tech minaret (a prototype section of which the V&A is collecting), which was a Huguenot church and then synagogue before becoming a mosque for the Bangladeshi diaspora; Old Kent Road Mosque, a conversion of a former pub serving a largely Nigerian community; and Harrow Central Mosque, which used to occupy a pair of semi-detached houses acquired by Pakistani immigrants, before a purpose-built mosque was constructed nearby to replace it. The exhibition presents 1:1 reconstructions of their highly decorative *mihrabs*, *minbars* and other architectural elements, and shows interviews with community members alongside films of the mosques in use, made by artist Julie Marsh in collaboration with their congregations. It shows how these self-built mosques are in a state of constant evolution, and documents and celebrates the unique visual language of Islam that has emerged in architecture in Britain.

The UK has 1,800 mosques catering to a community of more than 3 million Muslims. 'Religious congregations are independent and self-organised, and anyone can start a mosque, anywhere,' Saleem notes of these grass-roots, crowd-sourced, community projects. The majority are improvised and ad hoc, found in terraced houses, old libraries, and former cinemas and supermarkets, where they have adapted to and altered the British vernacular. They are deeply pragmatic, maximising every available space for prayer, and double up as vibrant community hubs, fulfilling a variety of functions beside worship. For example, my local mosque in Limehouse, east London, occupies three railway arches under the Docklands Light Railway. In one, there is a space to do one's ablutions, and in another the main prayer hall (the last is for the overspill). Worshippers have to pass between the arches on the pavement outside, as no internal doors are permitted. During busy Friday prayer, the congregation spills out on to the street, which is covered in special plastic matting for the occasion. Such mosques were self-built by the people who use them, designed by mosque committees in dialogue with local planning officials and residents, a process not without controversy. Rather than one culture being required to become like, or assimilate into, the other, these buildings reshape cities through a process of two-way integration, where both existing and new are invited to change.

These improvised mosques are embodiments of community ambition, and as they grow, congregations often fundraise to move to larger

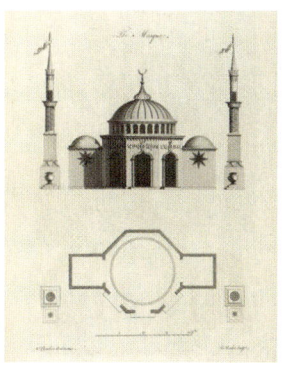

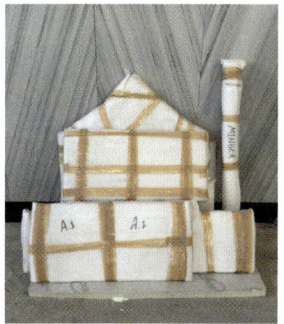

Top: Engraving of the Mosque Pavilion at Kew Gardens designed by William Chambers, 1761 © RIBA Collections

Bottom: An assemblage of the materials to be used to create the *mihrab* in the Baitul Aman Mosque in Bethnal Green, London

premises or to demolish these buildings and construct new, larger mosques in their place. By the entrance to many ad hoc mosques, where worshippers must take off their shoes, there is often a sizeable safe, intended for donations (or *fisabilillah*, which translates as 'for the sake of Allah') either to good works or to such building projects.

What is striking about these aspirations is how explicitly architectural they are, and several London mosques visited in the research for the Biennale exhibition had architectural renders and plans for these wished-for structures prominently displayed, sometimes accompanied by an itemised list of the costs, even pictures of 'possible sanitaryware', ablutions being an integral part of preparations for prayer. In Lewisham Mosque, for example, which occupies a row of former shops, plans by Saleem for a new mosque are on display in the prayer hall on a lockable display board. Below it is an accompanying bit of paper breaking down the £8,780,000 costs, including £200,000 to demolish the site and £300,000 to rent an alternative prayer space for the three years it would take to construct a replacement. The congregation is outgrowing the current arrangement, and every possible room is carpeted in a blue pile, banded to help worshippers orientate towards Makkah. The *mihrab* is made of laminate flooring and the space is divided with foldable partitions, decorated with Islamic motifs. In Forest Gate Mosque, there is another notice board, showing similar plans, with renders of the entrance to the proposed mosque and school that will grow on the site. If realised, it will be a large square building, with a portico and five tall, arched windows and a blue dome. 'We ask the *ummah* (community) to join us in this exciting journey,' one of the trustees explains: every Wednesday and Friday they raise money, with donations totalling £300 an evening, sometimes on a good night, after pay day, £1,000. This was bolstered when a community member sold a flat and donated the proceeds. Nevertheless, having raised £750,000 so far, they are some way off their £5 million target. At Old Kent Road Mosque, in a former pub called the Duke of Kent, a PVC banner has pictures showing the building's past, present and future along with a quote from the Prophet Muhammad: 'Whoever builds a mosque for Allah, then Allah will build him a house like it in paradise.' In the main prayer hall, there is a promotional video that shows the as yet unrealised designs; on a window ledge rests a bucket used for the fundraising campaign, decorated with an earlier iteration of the proposed mosque.

As a result of this evolution in mosque-making, improvised structures are being lost to the new-build projects that replace them. The Biennale exhibition documents a few of these structures before they disappear, with photographs and digital scans that captured this important but ephemeral

JOHN TANN'S
RELIANCE
LOCKS,
FIRE & BURGLAR-PROOF
SAFES,
IRON DOORS, ROOMS &c
WAREHOUSE 11, NEWGATE ST.
WORKS

moment in the evolution of the British mosque. There has been a corresponding flourishing of purpose-built mosques, the fruition of decades of iterative developments in mosque architecture. Many of these repudiate Glancey's negative judgment but also see his aspiration for British mosque architecture starting to be realised. Examples include Saleem's mosques, which incorporate abstracted patterns from Islamic art into contemporary designs; Mangera Yvars' forthcoming North Harrow Community Centre; and the new £23 million Cambridge Central Mosque by Marks Barfield Architects, with its internal forest of CNC-milled columns, which bills itself as 'Europe's first eco-mosque'.

Cambridge Mosque architect Julia Barfield's great-grandfather, Sir Thomas Arnold, a British Orientalist who taught philosophy at the Mohammedan Anglo-Oriental College in Aligarh, India, was a trustee of the Woking mosque, which Glancey so admires. Barfield did not know this coincidence until, working on the Cambridge commission, she read Saleem's book. Arnold, who was a mentor of the celebrated Pakistani poet, Sir Muhammad Iqbal, was also secretary of the committee that established the East London Mosque, which occupied premises on Commercial Road before moving to Whitechapel in 1975. These new mosque buildings are designed to be culturally porous, intended as spaces that feel welcoming to people of all faiths, and eschew minarets, which in the UK are purely symbolic (East London Mosque is one of the few allowed to broadcast the call to prayer). They are trying to find a new language of mosque architecture that fuses the contemporary with the traditional and is in deliberate dialogue with the local vernacular. They ask the fundamental question: what should a British mosque be in the twenty-first century?

'The new Cambridge Mosque shifts the narrative of mosque architecture in Britain,' says Saleem, writing in *The RIBA Journal* of May 2019. 'Driven by an ambition of intercultural exchange and dialogue, it is the architecture of hope, and if it succeeds it may come to be seen as one of the most significant religious buildings in Britain of a generation.' Islamophobia and far-right violence are on the rise in Britain. In the last few years, five mosques in Birmingham have had their windows broken on the same night, Manchester Nasfat Islamic Centre has been gutted by an arson attack, a van was driven into a crowd leaving Finsbury Park Mosque, and an imam was murdered by a white extremist at the London Central Mosque in Regent's Park. A recent YouGov poll commissioned by the Muslim Council of Britain found that almost ninety per cent of Britons have never visited a mosque. The Ramadan and Venice Pavilions, by inviting visitors to explore mosque architecture and appreciate its contribution to the British urban landscape and architectural history, will hopefully encourage more to cross the threshold.

Top: The Shahporan Mosque in east London, designed by Makespace Architects, a new-build and house-mosque combined

Bottom: Interior of Cambridge Central Mosque, designed by Marks Barfield Architects
© Morley von Sternberg

The Ramadan Pavilion

Christopher Turner
Shahed Saleem

The Ramadan Pavilion
Christopher Turner
Shahed Saleem

CT   The Ramadan Pavilion was inspired by an eighteenth-century folly built by William Chambers at Kew Gardens, which was the first mosque structure in Britain. It was an Orientalist fantasy, rather than a functioning mosque. How does your own pavilion reference and update this structure while avoiding such a romanticisation of the East, with all the patronising, imperial power dynamics that involves?

SS   The folly at Kew was a symbol of the Muslim world as it was being experienced by Europeans in the eighteenth century through the asymmetric power relations of trade and colonisation. It was an Orientalising vision, detached from any real experience of the culture that it was representing. It compressed Muslim history into an easily recognisable image and established the trope of the mosque as a building with a dome and minarets.
   The Ramadan Pavilion is the post-colonial to Chambers' colonial representation. Rather than symbolising a culture that is distant and exotic, it is about a community that is an integral part of Britain's composition. From the 1960s, there was large-scale Muslim migration into Britain from her former colonies. As these newcomers settled, they established mosques, first in adapted houses and other buildings, then in purpose-built structures.
   This pavilion is a celebration of the Islamic architecture that they have built, from ad hoc conversions to new buildings with multiple historical references. It represents this Muslim diaspora's architectural history, how they envisage themselves in Britain and how they seek to connect with the wider Muslim world and its history.

CT   The Victoria and Albert Museum was founded with the proceeds from the 1851 Great Exhibition, and opened in 1857, the year that the Indian Rebellion was brutally suppressed; the following year the British government took over control of the country from the East India Company, founding the Raj. The museum's South Asian collections have their origins in the East India Company's museum, or Oriental Depository (which, after 1858, became the India Museum). How does your pavilion – and indeed your mosque designs – reference the V&A's eclectic Islamic collection?

SS   Muslims in Britain have created an architectural language that references historic Islamic art and architecture in a host of different ways – sometimes through direct replicas, sometimes through approximations. Much of this referencing is made possible through material held in museums and reproduced in images. I have used the V&A collection to find historic references for my own work, in particular for the mosque I designed in east London, which takes its inspiration from a series of thirteenth-century tiles from an Anatolian palace complex on display in the Jameel Gallery. I used this as the motif for the facade of the mosque, adapting its scale and shape to turn it into a more abstract building element.

The Ramadan Pavilion deliberately references [Victorian architect and designer] Owen Jones's Islamic-inspired geometric designs and K.A.C. Creswell's early twentieth-century photographs of Cairene mosques. This illustrates the point that the architecture of British Islam draws from many different sources of Islamic history, and that many of these representations have come through European engagement with the Muslim world.

However, the pavilion is about those who have traditionally been the silent subject of European representations, now post-colonial and taking ownership of their own image, and projecting it into a significant cultural institution such as the V&A, itself born in the colonial period from which those representations sprung. It raises questions about the power of representation, who is the author and who the subject, and who controls our cultural narratives.

CT   The Ismaili Centre, opposite the museum, includes a rooftop charbagh garden, based on the four gardens of Paradise mentioned in the Qur'an. On a recent tour, my guide gestured at the V&A's roof, visible over a wall, and said: 'We don't have a dome, so we had to borrow yours'. Can you describe how your pavilion riffs on elements of the V&A's South Kensington building?

SS   I have designed the pavilion to be a reconfigured assemblage of architectural elements that are either overtly Islamic, such as the minaret and *minbar*, or have dual identities, as I feel that this is how Muslims in Britain negotiate their own place in society. So, the dome of the pavilion could echo a mosque dome, but it is styled on the profile of the V&A dome. The arches are again a familiar trope of Islamic architecture, but here they replicate the windows surrounding the courtyard. Some of the fretwork in the collections has also been used as references, for example in the truss and the screen walls. In this way, the idea of the British mosque as a collection of borrowed objects and signs is embodied in the pavilion.

CT   The pavilion is intended to host 'Open Iftar' events during Ramadan. Can you explain the importance of your temporary structure as a focal point for British Muslims in this holy month, and in breaking-of-the-fast events?

SS   Ramadan is the holiest month in the Muslim calendar and has many spiritual benefits associated with it. It was the month in which the Prophet Muhammad would fast and seclude himself, and it was in this month that the Qur'an started to be revealed to him. For Muslims to be able to celebrate this month so publicly and in such a festive and positive way will be of huge significance for a community that spends much of its time feeling embattled by media representations. It will be a positive force in the short term and will have longer lasting impacts that we won't see straight away. To have an event significant to Muslim religion

26　A computer visualisation of the Ramadan Pavilion installed at the V&A

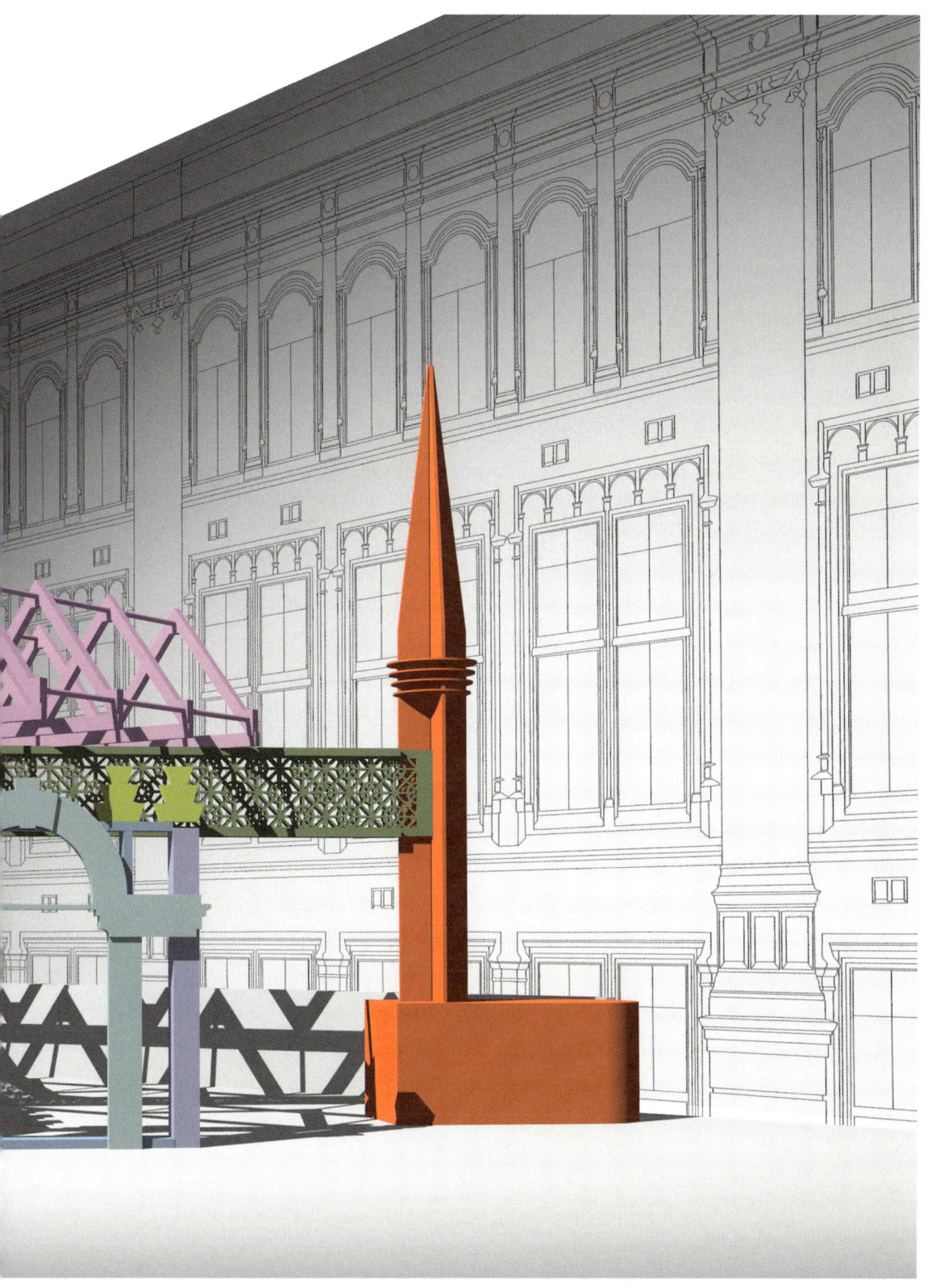

and culture in a major museum brings huge visibility and recognition to a community that does not feel that it has access to, or belong in, such places. It will change the way people perceive and experience Muslim culture, but also how Muslims relate to the V&A.

CT   How does the pavilion make a comment on the architecture of British mosques more generally, specifically the ad hoc mosques that have adapted to and changed the urban landscape of Britain?

SS   The number of mosques in Britain has been growing exponentially since the 1960s and perhaps eighty per cent of these have been created through the adaptation of existing buildings, often self-designed by the communities that use them. It is a typology where, through improvisation and appropriation, a new architectural language has emerged. These mosques both integrate with and challenge existing architectural and cultural norms, and I think they are really unique types of architecture in this country.
    Communities often aspire to replace these ad hoc structures with purpose-built mosques. Probably most mosque-building now involves replacing converted buildings with new-builds, although some mosques are still being established in adapted spaces. The improvised is, perhaps by its nature, a temporary stage. The pavilion takes this ethos of British mosque architecture, as a fluid assemblage of local and historical references, and celebrates it in a festive and expressive way.

CT   The exhibition at the Venice Architecture Biennale explores three such case studies of mosques created through the adaptation of existing buildings, and the Ramadan Pavilion is intended to act as a bridge between London and the Veneto, engaging those not able to travel to Italy. How do the two projects complement and relate to each other?

SS   Our Venice Biennale exhibition is a careful documentation of the key architectural elements of the three London mosques, illustrating the way in which British mosques have been created in the post-war period. It tells the detailed story of a type of architecture, of which the Ramadan Pavilion is a more abstracted and joyous expression.
    This period of mosque architecture will eventually pass, as the adapted buildings and self-made aesthetics give way to more intentionally designed and off-the-shelf structures. Both the exhibition and the pavilion are about identifying, representing and recording this point in the history not only of the mosque, but of religious architecture in Britain – celebrating it before it is lost forever, but accepting that it is part of an aspirational journey.

Perth, 2018

Birmingham, 2014

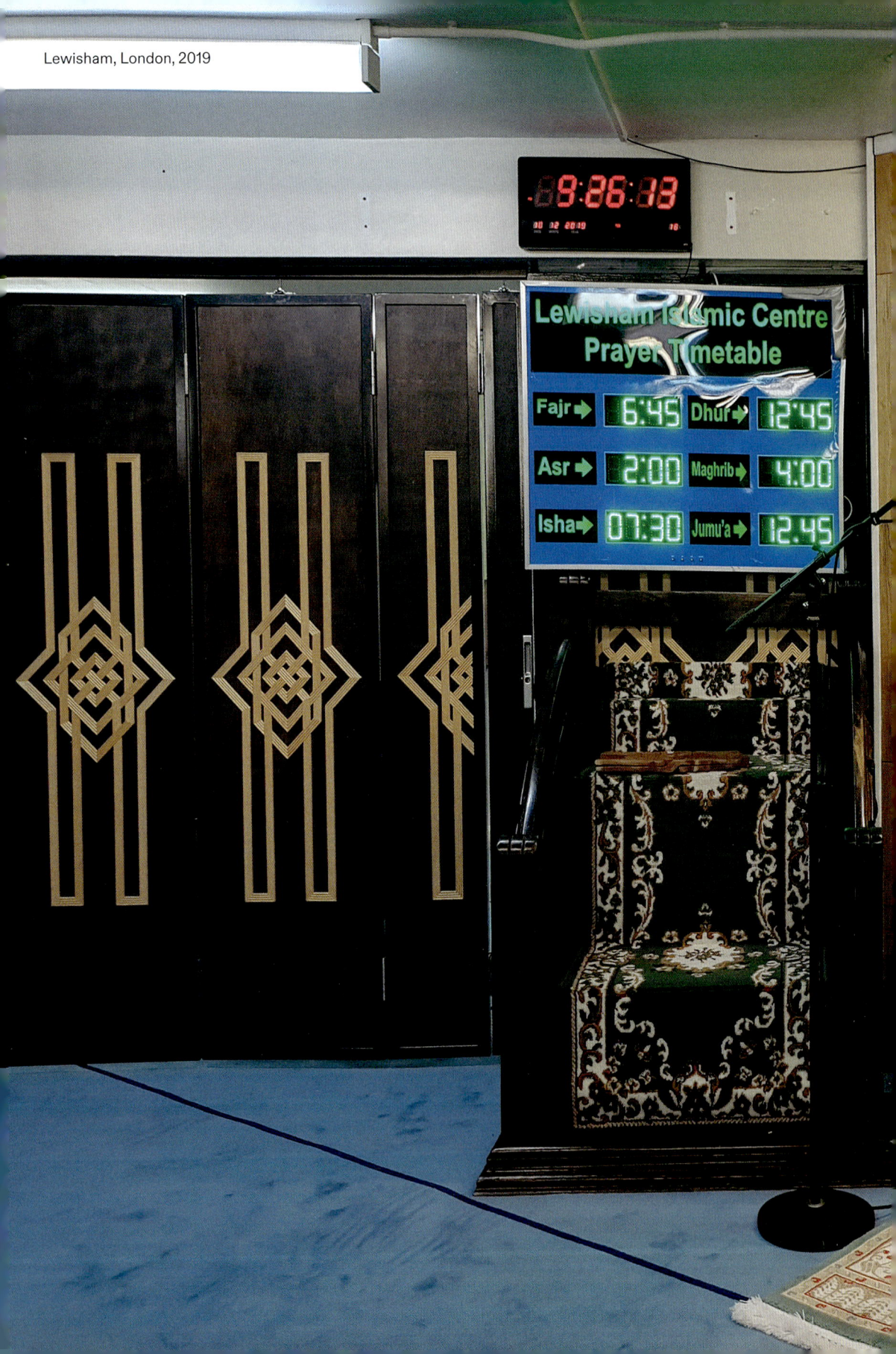

Lewisham, London, 2019

Swansea, 2018

Regent's Park, London, 2013

Documenting the mosque in the V&A Collections

Ella Kilgallon

Documenting the mosque in the V&A Collections
Ella Kilgallon

In 2019, the Victoria and Albert Museum acquired a collection of sketches and travel sketchbooks by Shahed Saleem (museum nos. E.1046 to 1049-2019). A number of his sketches are a visual exploration of the typology of the mosque, inspired by examples of Islamic architecture encountered by Saleem on his travels, both in the UK and abroad. It was the acquisition of these sketches, in part prompted by a recognition of the absence of British Islam in the V&A's collection, that developed into the wider British Mosques project. Within these colourful sketches, drawn in pen, with wash and felt tip added later, the architectural features of the mosque are isolated, combined and re-imagined in new and provocative ways. Saleem's sketchbooks are in some ways a continuation of the tradition of sketchbooks made by travellers to the Muslim world, of which the V&A has a large collection, but they are also a meaningful departure. As a British-born Muslim of migrant parents, Saleem's sketches offer a new perspective on Islamic architecture in a British and global context.

Record sketches, drawings and photographs made by European travellers to the Islamic world have been part of the museum's collection since its foundation, in part due to a small group of architects closely connected to the Government School of Design and the South Kensington Museum (which became the V&A in 1899). Owen Jones (1809-74) and James Wild (1814-92) in particular were instrumental in inspiring a British interest in architecture from the Islamic world, promoting its polychromatic decoration in opposition to the neutral colours of neo-classical styles popular at the time. Their close connection to the South Kensington Museum, as architects and art advisors, resulted in an important group of drawings and architectural fragments entering the collection that document a European perspective on what is broadly termed Islamic art and architecture. This all-encompassing term was, and still is, used for works made in vastly different geographical regions where Islam is the faith of the majority of the population. 'Islamic' incorporates both religious and secular art spanning some 1,400 years. Although the term encompasses far-reaching territories, it was the countries of the Ottoman Empire, including Turkey, Syria and Egypt, that were most connected with Europe – outside of the remains of al-Andalus in Spain. Diplomatic and trade relations between Europe and the Ottoman Empire facilitated travel and, as a result, the majority of mosques represented in the V&A's collections are from these regions.

One of the greatest British design theorists of the nineteenth century, Owen Jones was heavily inspired by the architecture he encountered on his travels to Egypt, Turkey and Spain. His study of the Alhambra in Granada, a fortified palace complex built by the Nasrid dynasty (1232-1492) during the last period of Muslim rule in Spain, became one of the most influential British books on Islamic architecture. Among the book's admirers was Henry Cole, chief advisor for the Great Exhibition of 1851 and the first director of the South Kensington Museum. Cole commissioned Jones to design the interiors of the Great Exhibition venue, the Crystal

Painted sketch illustrating how mosques are experienced in the townscape by Shahed Saleem, 2015.
© Victoria and Albert Museum, London. Museum no. E.1047-2019

Palace, inspired by his study of the Alhambra. In the course of the Exhibition, Jones joined the committee responsible for choosing objects from the event for the School of Design collection, which became the core of the South Kensington Museum. As well as being instrumental in selecting objects, Jones's own architectural studies of the Alhambra and of the sixteenth-century Süleymaniye Mosque in Istanbul formed an early part of the collection (museum nos. 8271-8277; 9156A-O).

The ideas that Jones began to develop in his study of the Alhambra were fully realised in *The Grammar of Ornament,* the design manual he published in 1856. In an attempt to synthesise both the industrial and imperial ethos of the period, Jones gathered and analysed ornament from around the world. Decorative examples from Cairo, Turkey, Andalusia, Iran and India were documented with varying degrees of detail. The chapter on 'Arabian ornament' focused solely on examples from Cairo, predominantly the mosques of Ibn Tulun (referred to as Tooloon), Qalawun (Kalaoon) and al-Nasir Muhammad (En Nasireeyeh), and was indebted to James Wild, who had spent time in Cairo in the 1840s carrying out detailed studies of domestic and religious architecture. An extraordinary piece of work containing 100 chromolithograph plates, *The Grammar of Ornament* was an attempt to create a set of universal design principles. Its approach also helped to shape the South Kensington Museum's collecting policies. The museum's significant collection of mosque lamps and Islamic ceramics, acquired throughout the late nineteenth century, served as examples of ornament. Extracted from their religious and cultural context, they were appreciated as designed objects from which to draw inspiration.

Following similar principles, in 1869 the South Kensington Museum acquired a collection of architectural elements from Egyptian buildings of the Mamluk period. Originally sent to Paris by the Egyptian government for display during the 1867 international exhibition, the pieces were subsequently sold to the museum by Husayn Fahmi al-Mi'mar, a senior official in the Egyptian administration referred to in Europe as 'Dr Meymar'. Among the group of objects purchased was a largely complete *minbar* made for Sultan Qaytbay between 1468 and 1496 (museum no. 1050:1 to 2-1869) and a collection of carved wooden plaques from the *minbar* of Sultan Husam al-Din Lajin (ruler between 1296 and 1299) made for the mosque

Top: Original drawing for 'Moresque No. 4. Plate XLII' of *The Grammar of Ornament* by Owen Jones, published 1856. © Victoria and Albert Museum, London. Museum no. 1615

Bottom: Section drawing from the Süleymaniye Mosque, Istanbul (built 1550-57), by Owen Jones, 1809-74. © Victoria and Albert Museum, London. Museum no. 8267A

of Ibn Tulun in Cairo (museum nos. 1051 to 1052-1869; 1085:1 to 9-1869). Both objects are striking examples of Mamluk geometric designs created with intricately carved wood panels. The significance of these architectural fragments was well known to Wild, who had studied the mosques' interiors while in Cairo in the 1840s. When the plaques of the Lajin *minbar* arrived at the museum in 1869, Wild helped to reconstruct their original arrangement based on a measured drawing he had made years earlier. Wild's study of the *minbar*, included in one of nine sketchbooks from his travels in Egypt, was donated to the V&A in 1938 (museum no. E.3841-1938). The complete *minbar* of Sultan Qaytbay and plaques from the Lajin *minbar* are on display in the Jameel Gallery at the V&A.

The interest in Islamic and Islamic-inspired design evident in the early years of the South Kensington Museum reflected the wider interest of artists and architects alert to the culture of the Muslim world through European colonial and trade networks. Separating the cultural and religious context from the art and architecture they studied, artists often romanticised and exoticised the daily life they encountered. A collection of more than 2,000 drawings documenting the Middle East and North Africa came to the V&A from the British collector, Rodney Searight (1909-91). Purchased in 1985, the collection is witness to British and foreign artists and travellers who visited these regions between 1750 and 1900. Searight worked and lived for many years in Egypt and was an avid collector of paintings and drawings from the area. The collection he amassed is a combination of documentary and quotidian sketches, as well as fictitious scenes drawn from a Western, colonial imagination. These scenes frequently depict a passive and often sexualised culture, most apparent in the rendering of the *harem* (the female space within the household). Mosques were among the sites recorded through artists' views, such as John Frederick Lewis's interior view of the mosque of Hagia Sophia, Istanbul, painted between 1840 and 1841 (museum no. SD.582). Recording the eastern end of the Hagia Sophia (initially built as a church in 537 CE), the view details the *minbar* and painted plaques known as *levhas*, which bear the names of the Prophet Muhammad and the four successor 'caliphs' who were venerated by Sunni Muslims. Lewis was one of a number of nineteenth-century artists who travelled to Turkey and Egypt, recording the architecture, topography and people they encountered. Lewis himself lived in Cairo for ten years.

Objects documenting mosque architecture have entered the V&A's collections in various forms, including souvenirs. A small collection of carved sandalwood models, made around 1800-55, record the features of the Ahmedabad mosques of western India. Providing a rare representation of interior features, the *minbar* and *mihrab* of the fifteenth-century Muhafiz Khan Mosque are rendered in fine detail (museum nos. 01125 (IS); 01126 (IS)), and *jali* window screens from an unknown mosque are each carved with different tracery work (museum no. 01130:1-4 (IS)). Tabletop models of mosque buildings and their features were made in the Indian subcontinent for British officers of the East India Company. While largely produced as souvenirs, models were occasionally made for display at world expositions, at which India was represented by the

Photograph of the *mihrab* of the mosque of Mamluk Amir Aqsunqur al-Nasiri, Blue Mosque, Cairo (built 1346-47), by K.A.C. Creswell, 1916-21. © Victoria and Albert Museum, London. Museum no. 1601-1921

Photograph of the *minbar* of Mamluk Sultan al-Ashraf Qaytbay on display at the Victoria and Albert Museum, about 1913.
© Victoria and Albert Museum, London. Museum no. 1580-1913

Photograph of the Dome of the Rock, Jerusalem (originally built 688-92), by Francis Bedford, 1862. © Victoria and Albert Museum, London. Museum no. 53694

East India Company. At the international exposition of 1855 held in Paris, a model of a mosque was displayed alongside Hindu temples in the India section. While these models were not necessarily intended as an accurate architectural record, they record details now lost or damaged, such as the preaching platform of the Muhafiz Khan *minbar*, which had disappeared by 1900. The group of models in the V&A's collection were originally part of the India Museum established by the East India Company (1600-1858). Following its transfer to the British Government's India Office in 1858, the collection was eventually dispersed in 1879 to a number of institutions, including the V&A.

While mosque fragments and models make up a significant part of the collection, photographs are the largest source for mosque architecture collected by the South Kensington Museum. From its early iteration in 1852, the museum regarded photographic collections as an essential resource for students and artists, and began to amass works by photographers from around the world. Among some of the earliest photographs to enter the collection were those taken by Francis Bedford (1815-94) while on a royal tour from Cairo to Constantinople in 1862. The tour that Bedford carried out was a common extension to the Grand Tour circuit undertaken as part of the educational training of young gentlemen. From Venice or Naples, access to Greece and the Ottoman Empire was well established and British travellers had taken this route since the seventeenth century. Included in the group of Bedford's photographs acquired by the museum are records of a number of mosques: the Mosque of Muhammad Ali in Cairo (museum nos. 53650 and 53644), the Great Mosque in Damascus (museum no. 53741) and the Dome of the Rock in Jerusalem (museum no. 53694), where Bedford was one of only a small number of photographers granted special permission to access the site.

In 1920, the V&A began to acquire what would become one of its largest collections of photographs of Islamic architecture, from the scholar of medieval Islamic architectural history, K.A.C. Creswell (1879-1974). Born and educated in London, Creswell travelled to the Middle East in the First World War and subsequently worked as inspector of monuments in Syria and Palestine, before settling in Egypt. As part of his research, Creswell both acquired photographs of architectural sites and took and developed his own. These illustrated his monographs: *Early Muslim Architecture* (1932, 1940) and *The Muslim Architecture of Egypt* (1952, 1959), written under the patronage of King Fuad I and his son King Farouq of Egypt. Creswell wrote to the V&A in 1920 about his collection of photographs, and the museum became the first public collection to acquire a set, purchasing more throughout the 1920s and 30s. A total of more than 3,000 prints documenting the Islamic architecture of Egypt, Syria, Palestine, Jordan, Iraq, Tunisia and Turkey entered the museum's collection. Among the photographs are important records of monuments now lost, such as the *minbar* of Salah al-Din in the al-Aqsa Mosque, Jerusalem, destroyed by arson attack in 1969 (museum no. 2761-1921), and the minaret of the Umayyad Mosque, Aleppo, destroyed during the Syrian civil war in 2013 (museum no. 2351-1921).

Intended as a global sourcebook of inspiration for students of design and manufacture, the V&A has collected the architecture of the mosque in many (although certainly not all) of its varied forms, since its foundation. The early collection represents both a fragmentary and idealised understanding of the Muslim world as encountered by Europeans and mediated through objects, photographs and drawings. Shahed Saleem, in his research on the British mosque, has questioned whether mosque-making in Britain has involved a similar process of mediation. Embedded in the history of colonialism and migration, British mosques of the mid-twentieth century were fashioned through imported cultural references from across the Muslim world. These community-designed spaces are testament to the formative years of Islam in Britain. The V&A is set to acquire the 3D scans of a number of London mosques made between the 1970s and 90s by converting existing buildings into places of worship. Made by the University of Westminster, the scans are an attempt to systematically document the buildings and their complex cultural references. The tradition of collecting architectural fragments also continues with the acquisition of test pieces made for the Brick Lane Mosque minaret in 2009. Steel-cut and designed to be filled with LED lights, the minaret is an example of contemporary mosque architecture that embraces the High Tech. Once part of the V&A's collection, the scans and minaret test pieces will form a continuation of, as well as a counterpoint to, the museum's historic collections that document and represent the diverse architecture of the global mosque.

Tracing the elements of the British mosque

Shahed Saleem

Tracing the elements of the British mosque
Shahed Saleem

The first mosques in Britain both date from 1889, one a converted Georgian terraced house in the northern port city of Liverpool, and the other in Woking, south of London, a purpose-built building designed in an expressive style referencing historic motifs of Muslim architecture. These two buildings encapsulate much of the story of the mosque in Britain. The house-mosque was established by an emerging local Muslim community, in this case of English converts to Islam, and was adapted from domestic to religious space. There were no external alterations, but a prayer hall was built at the rear and the interior was fitted out with features and decoration styled on the traditional Islamic architecture of North Africa. The mosque at Woking, commissioned by a Jewish Hungarian linguist who had lived in northern India, was the Orientalist vision of an exotic Islamic culture expressed in a flamboyant visual language.

By the mid-twentieth century, there were only four further mosques across the country, mostly located in port cities, where Muslims from Bengal, Yemen and Somalia who had laboured on shipping routes were forming settled communities. The decades after the independence and partition of India in 1947 saw large-scale Muslim migration from South Asia into Britain's cities and the establishment and growth of significant Muslim populations. From the 1970s onwards, these early migrants were joined by further Muslim migration, also the fallout of decolonisation, from across Africa, the Middle East and South-east Asia. Added to significant numbers of white and Afro-Caribbean Muslim converts, Britain could most likely boast the world's most diverse Muslim population. By 2018, Muslims had become the largest minority religion in the country, with a population of 3.4 million, of which over half traced their origins to Pakistan, India or Bangladesh and the remainder from across the Muslim world.

Finding themselves in a new, strange and hostile environment, these Muslim communities naturally coalesced along ethnic lines, where language, culture and histories were shared. They quickly felt the need to reconstruct the social and religious culture that they had left behind and were dislocated from. The mosque was a primary means through which to do this; it was a vehicle around which a community could coalesce and through which their collective religious and cultural identity could be established anew. Mosque-building, therefore, proliferated across Britain in the second half of the twentieth century, from the handful that existed in 1960 to approximately 1,800 today.

The mosque has a very simple programme. In essence, it is simply a space where a congregation can pray facing the house of God, the Ka'bah in Makkah, and requires nothing other than this direction (the *qibla*). The first mosque was that of the Prophet Muhammad in Medina in the early seventh century. It was a courtyard with his living quarters around, with one of the walls marking the direction of prayer. The Prophet was the imam, and would lead the prayer, standing at the front facing Makkah, and the congregation would line up in neat rows behind him, men at the front and women behind.

Top: 8 Brougham Terrace, Liverpool, which was converted into Britain's first mosque in 1889

Bottom: Prayer in the East London Mosque, 2016

The key elements that have come to symbolise the prayer space of the mosque in every part of the world are the *mihrab*, the niche from where the imam leads the prayer, the *minbar*, a pulpit for sermons, and the row carpet. The first two have their origins in the Prophet's mosque of the early seventh century. Oludamini Ogunnaike writing in *The Art of Orientation* (2021) describes how this *mihrab* may have been a simple stone slab or sign on the wall to indicate the direction of prayer. There are also symbolic interpretations based on the etymology of the Arabic word *mihrab*, that it represents a place from which a struggle against the ego is waged. Alongside this, based on pre-Islamic poetry and Qur'anic references, the *mihrab* is also understood as a sanctuary from where worship takes place. The *mihrab* as a niche emerged in later renovations of the Prophet's mosque, and has a number of pre-Islamic antecedents, such as palaces, Byzantine churches and Greco-Roman temples.

The *minbar* also has its origins in the mosque of the Prophet, specifically the two steps and a seat from which he would preach to the congregation. As Islam spread, the *minbar* evolved distinct forms and characteristics in each region that the religion established itself. They were mostly made of wood, though stone and marble examples are also found, and were usually elaborately decorated. In larger mosques in some cultures, such as Egypt and the Ottoman Empire, the *minbar* became quite tall, more like a flight of stairs than a pulpit, and could be adorned with canopies and portals.

The Prophet's mosque did not have carpets or rugs but the ground was covered with sand and small pebbles. Woollen carpets are thought to have appeared in the early centuries of Islam, although the row carpets that are now familiar came later. These emerged as single-niche prayer carpets for use in mosques, palaces and homes, evolving into multi-row prayer carpets with several niches to accommodate more people, the earliest examples of which date from the fifteenth century.

As new geographies were absorbed into the Muslim world, their cultures fused with Islamic art and architecture to create new and emergent visual languages. Geometric decoration, calligraphy, row carpets, vaulted arches, domes and minarets were the grammar from which each region developed its own particular Islamic style. Northern Europe and Britain, those former colonial homelands where Muslims

The *mihrab*, *minbar* and *qibla* wall of the new prayer hall at Shah Jahan Mosque, Woking, 2018

established significant diasporic communities, were no exception to this artistic spread of Islam.

As Muslim migrants in Britain started to create their own mosques from the 1960s, this was the architectural and artistic history to which they referred, often drawing from their own memories of the Islamic architectures of their countries of origin, mixed with media images in books, magazines and television. These early mosques were set up in adapted buildings, often houses, by local communities who self-organised to raise funds among themselves, find properties and carry out rudimentary, ad hoc conversions. Without any precedents or blueprints for this type of adaptation, they had to find inventive ways to adorn these buildings as places of Muslim worship. A new religious typology, the self-made and improvised mosque, emerged, bringing with it a new visual culture, and became widespread across the country.

These mosques established and institutionalised the public practice of Muslim prayer in Britain for the first time. Five prayers are spread throughout the day, from sunrise to sunset, and these can be performed individually or in congregation. The mosques became a place where the five congregational prayers would take place, with the Friday midday prayer being the most significant of the week. In addition to this, the mosques established core activities such as religious education for

Top: Prayer timings displayed digitally in Folkstone Mosque, 2019

Middle: A framed photograph of Makkah in the London Central Mosque, 2013

Bottom: A calligraphic wall piece waiting to be hung at Baitul Aman Mosque, Bethnal Green, London, 2019

children and funerals. As the mosques became more established and as communities grew, the range of services expanded to encompass wider social and community activities.

With Muslim populations rapidly increasing, the mosques had to keep adapting and extending to accommodate their growing congregations. In a number of cases, a mosque that had started as an adapted building, and had been extended as far as possible, would be replaced with a newly built mosque either on the same site or nearby. These purpose-built mosques started emerging in larger numbers from the 1980s onwards but overall have remained the minority. Some eighty per cent of British mosques today have been formed through the adaptation and alteration of existing buildings. These are not only houses but also a host of other building types: cinemas, banks, public houses, factories, offices, libraries, and so on. The mosque in Britain, therefore, is a typology of the adaptation and improvisation of found space.

In these adaptations, the *mihrab* and *minbar* have been expressed in various ways, and with reference to a range of Islamic traditions as well as invented approaches. In some cases, where mosques are large and purpose-built, a tall free-standing ornamental staircase has been installed, but most have remained smaller structures of a few steps with varied styles of decoration. The *mihrab* has usually been more elaborate, serving as the most prominent architectural feature within the prayer hall. It has offered an opportunity for Islamic signification and, as such, has become an important expressive device, whether it be plain or ornamental. In Britain, the *mihrab* has varied from the self-made, fashioned from everyday building materials, to large and elaborate constructions, sometimes replicating examples from across Muslim history. Not all mosques, however, have a *mihrab* at all. Some have omitted it on the basis that it is a decorative element and therefore unnecessary to, and detracting from, the purpose of prayer. For others, it may not have been possible to build one for cost reasons. The *mihrab* and *minbar* have often formed part of an arrangement on the *qibla* wall, which might include other signifying features such as calligraphy and images of the holy cities of Makkah and Medina, as well as an array of clocks. These clocks would show the prayer times as they change from day to day. More recently, the prayer times would be displayed on digital screens, which might also display other information relating to the mosque's activities.

Muslim prayer is a highly embodied practice, in which shoes are removed to undertake a series of standing and sitting postures accompanied by recitations in Arabic. The mosque carpet, therefore, has become central to this experience. In the early days, there was no access to mosque carpet manufacturers, so standard domestic carpets would be adapted with tape or pen, marking out the rows where worshippers should stand and the direction they should face. As mosques were adapted from as-found buildings, the direction of Makkah was invariably skewed in these rooms, resulting in quirky visual geometries. As purpose-made mosque carpets became accessible, imported from Muslim countries, a range of patterns and styles came to adorn the floors of mosques, again in unusual alignments to the walls of the building. This misalignment became characteristic of the visual culture and experience of the mosque in Britain.

Although there is no religious requirement for the complete segregation of male and female in mosques, nevertheless most British mosques have separated the prayer spaces between the two. Where the women's prayer space was a separate room, a video link would be installed so the women could follow the prayer being led in the men's prayer hall. In some cases, the women's space would be on a gallery level overlooking the men's prayer hall, but this was usually in purpose-built mosques or larger converted buildings. Women's prayer spaces have always been smaller and plainer than the men's.

As mosques evolved in Britain, with purpose-built examples replacing adapted ones from the latter part of the twentieth century, they were increasingly designed professionally, with their architectural elements procured from suppliers in Muslim countries set up to provide for the diaspora. The earlier mosques established by post-war migrants, who self-designed and built them and brought Islamic references from their memories and lived experience, started to be replaced. Alongside this process, the Muslim population diversified and became increasingly British-born and, as tastes changed, so did the visual language of the mosque. In many cases, it became plainer, and where there was ornamentation it could be described as more refined and standardised, perhaps commercial even. The late decades of the twentieth century, when Islam was first publicly and comprehensively established as a religion in Britain by post-colonial migrants, therefore remains an important and unique phase in the history of the British mosque. Through the determination and resilience of this migrant generation, who brought with them a design culture and history spanning centuries and geographies, a new religious building type emerged.

Cardiff, 2013

East Ham, London, 2015

Woking, 2013

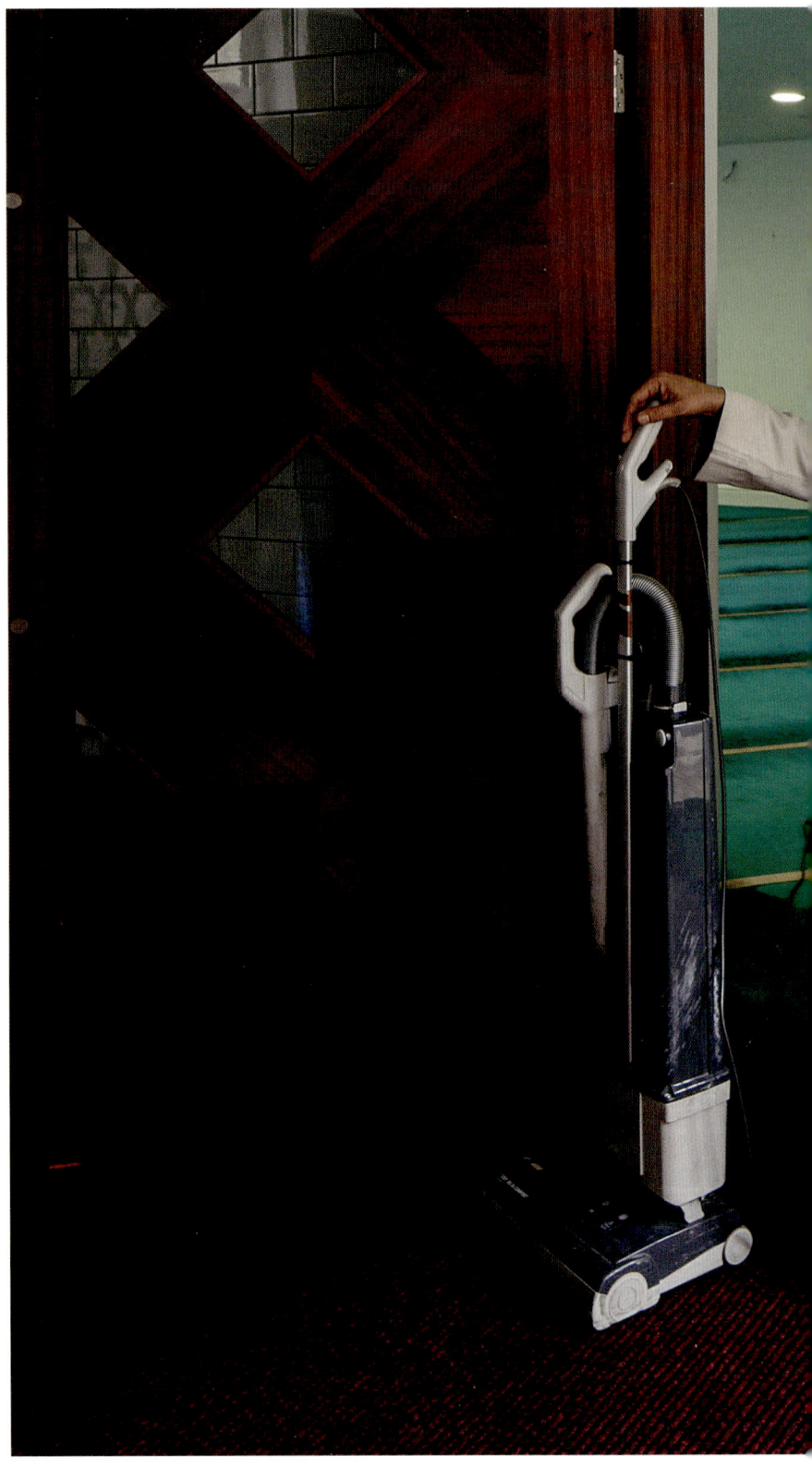

Bethnal Green, London, 2015

Old Kent Road, London, 2019

Brick Lane, London, 2020

Old Kent Road, London, 2019

Harrow, London, 2011

Brixton, London, 2016

Brick Lane, London, 2020

Bristol, 2013

Norwich, 2015

Old Kent Road, London, 2020

East Dulwich, London, 2017

Newcastle, 2013

Brick Lane, London, 2020

High Wycombe, 2013

Brick Lane, London, 2014

South Shields, 2014

Three British Mosques
Shahed Saleem
Christopher Turner
Ella Kilgallon

Mosques in Britain are grass-roots, crowd-sourced, community projects. In its simplest form, a mosque requires only a prayer hall and a *mihrab*, indicating the direction of prayer towards Makkah. There is no overarching religious authority that directs or funds mosque-building; religious congregations are independent and self-organised, and anyone can start a mosque, anywhere. The first mosque in Britain was created in 1889 by converting a terraced house in Liverpool, and there are now 1,800 mosques for the 3.4 million Muslims in the UK.

Mosques established by immigrant communities are often self-built and self-designed, responding to opportunity and community needs with an irreverent attitude to 'high' culture. They have adapted, and adapted to, British vernacular buildings, including terraced houses, pubs, cinemas, supermarkets and railway arches. References to global Islamic architecture are grafted onto the existing city, and through this a new material culture is born. Domes and pitched roofs are combined, minarets and gables juxtaposed, surfaces re-inscribed with arabesque patterns and calligraphy.

These mosques are in a continuous state of flux: as the community grows and its needs change, the buildings acquire numerous extensions and modifications. Often, they are eventually taken down to make way for new-build mosques – the results of some twenty or thirty years of organic and incremental growth. This significant period in the architectural history of Britain is largely undocumented and, as these sites are demolished, evidence of its existence will fade too.

Three British Mosques, the exhibition at the Pavilion of Applied Arts at the 17th International Architecture Exhibition of La Biennale di Venezia, is an attempt to document and illustrate the material culture of three mosques, each of which represents an important stage in the evolution of this typology. In addition to photography, 3D scans record the buildings in their current iterations. This is now the technology of choice for recording sites of heritage but is rarely used for hybrid buildings of this kind. Taken as a section through the building, the scans capture the interior layout, the relationship between the various spaces of the mosque, and the layers of adaptations.

In addition to the scans, key elements from each mosque are replicated at 1:1 scale. The extraction of these architectural fragments, from *mihrabs* to minarets, is a neat reversal of their insertion into the adapted buildings, and a fitting testament to their role in the creation of a new, hybrid British-Islamic architecture.

Case Study 1: Brick Lane Mosque

Existing places of worship, such as former churches and synagogues, were suited to conversion because they already contained a large prayer hall and often did not require extensive internal alteration. In 1976, the Bangladeshi Muslim community acquired such a building in the heart of east London. Built in 1743 as the Neuve Eglise, a Protestant chapel for Huguenot refugees, it became Spitalfields Great Synagogue in 1898 and, as local communities changed, was eventually sold for its new life as Brick Lane Mosque.

The migration of Bangladeshi communities into the East End started in the late nineteenth century when lascars (sailors) from Bengal, who served as labour on merchant shipping routes, began to settle near London's docks. After Britain's partition of India in 1947 and the consequent creation of Bangladesh in 1971, this migration increased. In 1998, the ward of Spitalfields was renamed Spitalfields and Banglatown in recognition of its majority Bangladeshi population.

Due to the heritage status of Brick Lane Mosque, the architectural ambitions of the Muslim community have been restricted. On the facade, the pediment retains its original Huguenot form, embellished by a central sundial (Figure 1) inscribed with a quote from Horace, the Latin motto *Umbra Sumus* – 'we are but shadow'. This reference to the passing of time has added significance considering the waves of Protestant, Jewish and Muslim migration to the East End.

The main hall, lit by a Venetian window on the east side, serves as the male prayer hall. Internal alterations were made to adapt the gallery into a second floor for additional prayer space. An eight-sided lightwell was created by repositioning the original Georgian panelling, allowing worshippers to see the *mihrab* below. To the right of the *mihrab* is the *minbar*, a set of steps with a platform, from which the imam delivers the Friday sermon. At Brick Lane, the *minbar* was designed with a Georgian pediment to reflect the room's original door cases (Figure 2).

One of the building's original wine cellars has been adapted to create a separate space for women to pray (Figure 3). In these vaulted rooms, which extend under the building and are accessed through a separate entrance, the female worshippers follow the prayer led by the imam in the main hall via a TV screen. Clocks on the wall indicate the daily prayer times.

In the attic are a series of classrooms originally constructed in 1897, when the building was a synagogue. The classrooms, which lead off a skylit central corridor, are now used to teach children Islamic studies and Arabic. Each classroom has a large dormer window, one of which has been used as a frame in which letters from the Arabic alphabet are placed to assist in teaching (Figure 4). In the central corridor, a stone tablet with a Hebrew inscription is testament to the building's earlier use.

After planning applications for the addition of minarets, finials and a dome were refused, permission was granted in 2009 for a 29m-high minaret structure. This was permitted on the condition that it was free-standing from the Georgian structure and taken down if the building ever stopped being used as a mosque. Positioned on a stone base, the stainless-steel structure is cut with an arabesque pattern and internally lit with coloured LEDs. The minaret is traditionally where the call to prayer is made, but in the UK it is generally symbolic, as speakers transmitting the call are not permitted. Designed by David Gallagher Architects, the minaret has become a landmark for east London.

Brick Lane Mosque is a testament to the changing cultural and religious demographic of east London. Within the building itself, these layers and adaptations are still visible. 3D scans of the structure, made to record the building in its current use, detail the many functions of the mosque, from the women's prayer space in the basement vaults, to the classrooms in the attic. The 3D scans and test pieces from the minaret form part of the exhibition at La Biennale di Venezia, and are being added to the V&A's collection as examples of contemporary British Islamic architecture.

> When I was 14 or 15, there were a lot of Jewish people living here. Sometimes they opened the synagogue and I would look at the door and wonder what was inside. So when our people bought this place in 1976, I entered the synagogue and looked at everything – at the culture, at the design. But our culture is Muslim so we painted, and we put down new things. We just had to leave the staircase and the door because it is heritage-listed. This is not empty land – if you see the East London Mosque or another mosque, they can change everything. But we can't change the building, we can just change certain things. Despite this, there has been a lot of change and now it looks like a mosque.

Al-haj Yousuf Kamaly, Brick Lane Mosque

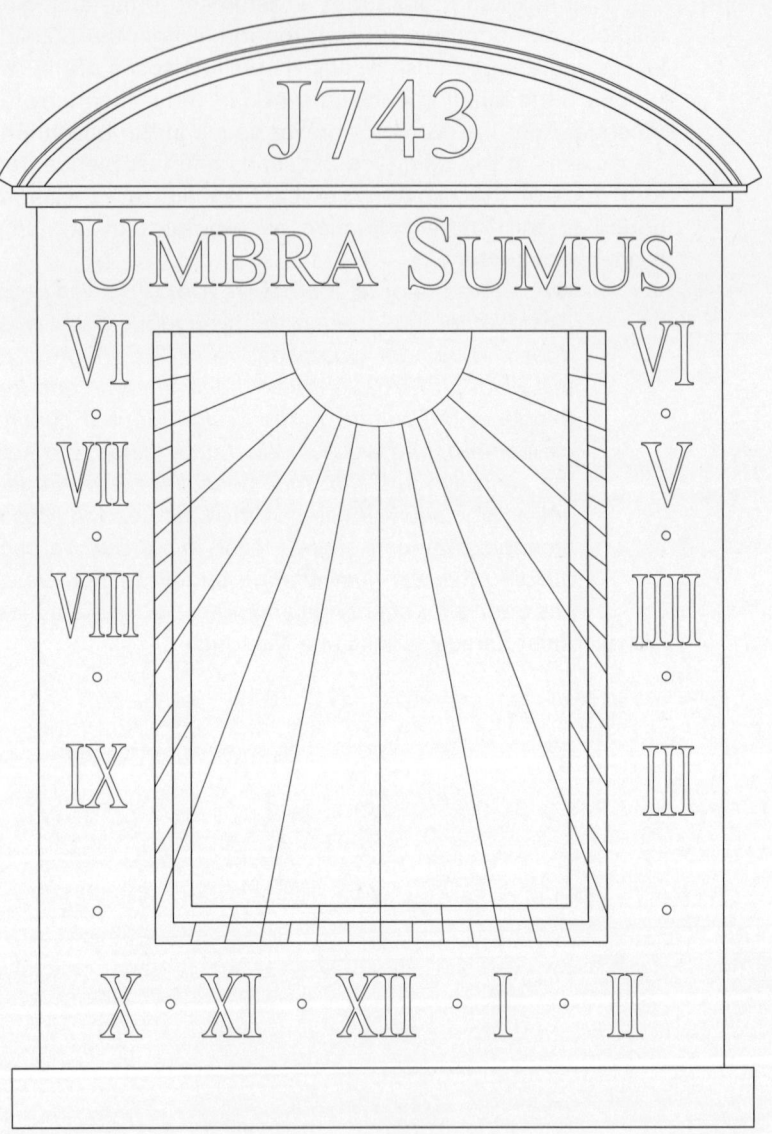

Figure 1: The Huguenot sundial on the south-facing pediment of the building

Figure 2: The *mihrab* in the main men's prayer hall

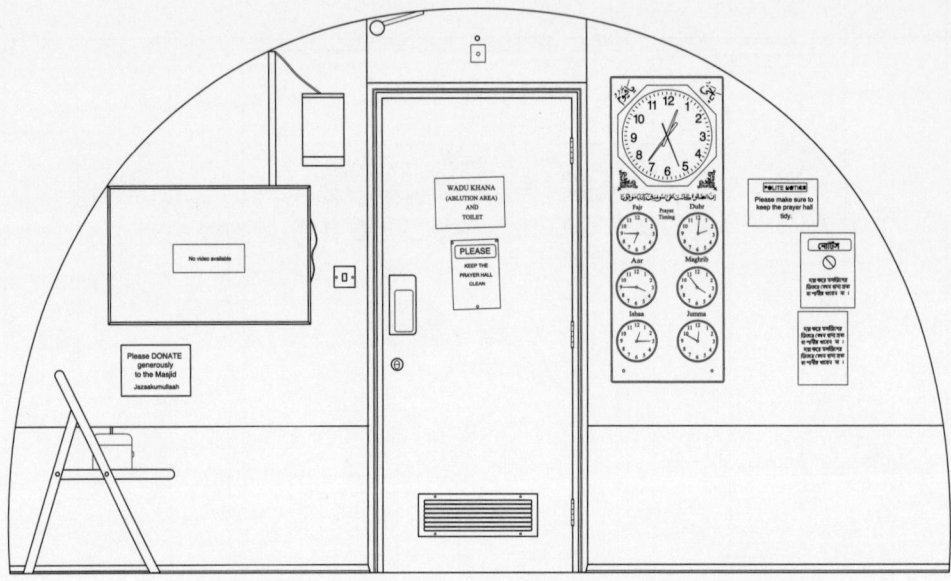

Figure 3: The end wall in the women's prayer room

Figure 4: Dormer window in one of the classrooms built in the roofspace of the mosque

Case Study 2: Old Kent Road Mosque

Libraries, cinemas, supermarkets, railway arches and pubs have all been repurposed by Muslim communities as places of worship. These adaptations vary widely, from subtle references, such as window embellishment, to the addition of prominent architectural features, like domes or minarets. In south London, home to the largest Nigerian population in Britain, a former Victorian pub in Southwark is now a mosque for the Muslim community.

The Duke of York on Old Kent Road was purchased in 1999 after years of fundraising by the Muslim Association of Nigeria, which was established in 1961 by a group of students living in London. Originally part of a row of terraced houses, the pub was derelict at the time. With changing community demographics, the function of the British pub has in many areas become obsolete. The building's two large rooms, once a dining room and a bar, were easily adapted to serve as prayer spaces. The upstairs dining room was converted into the main prayer hall and, directly below, the former bar became the women's prayer space. As separate entrances are also required, the male space is accessed from the back door.

The building is decorated throughout with accents of gold and green, which in many places highlight the pub's original interior ornament. The external window surrounds have been painted green, and dome motifs have been applied to the windows. The main prayer hall includes the *mihrab* and *minbar*. The *mihrab* is hand-painted in the same style as the rest of the prayer hall (Figure 5), and its form is echoed in the design of the row carpets. Behind the *minbar*, a frame contains the complete Qur'an in miniature type. The calligraphic wall inscription reads 'Allah', and is possibly styled on the circular panels, or *levhas*, in the mosque of the Hagia Sophia in Istanbul.

The mosque now serves a large and diverse Muslim community from south London and Kent, who are in the process of fundraising to replace the converted pub with a larger mosque building on the same site. In 2018, approval was granted for a six-storey mosque, incorporating three-storey arched windows and an abstracted minaret-liké structure. On the wall of the current mosque (Figure 6), a TV screen shows plans for the proposed building, a picture of which also appears on a fundraising bucket. Building a new mosque is both an act of devotion and the practical response of a growing community. Banners within the mosque quote a passage from the Prophet Muhammad that reads: "Whoever builds a mosque for Allah, then Allah will build him a house like it in paradise".

The Muslim community of Old Kent Road will rent a space nearby while construction work takes place. In the meantime, detailed 3D scans have captured the pub-mosque before it disappears, documenting a historic phase in the creative re-use of public buildings and their conversion to places of worship.

What I really love about this mosque is people having a voice, no matter what age they are, no matter where they're from, whether they're female or male. We have a stage downstairs where we have our sermon and we also hold lectures. We have a professor who gives the sermon – in Yoruba and English. He preaches the Qur'an and we can question him, we can challenge him. It's why I'm still here. For someone to sit on the stage and explain the Arabic in my language, in English, to both male and female, to me that's special.

Sideequah Dawodu, Old Kent Road Mosque

I think the new mosque will be a demonstration of all of the things that make us 'us'. It will be an outward display of the growth and influence of our community. Having a new building which is based on a community from Dulwich, Lewisham, Kent – all types of places – shows how far our reach has spread. It's important for people to see that we are a relevant community in 2021, and not just a small collection of people who do their own thing and don't grow and develop. Growth and development indicate success, and if people see that Muslims can be successful, it shows that we are viable members of this community.

Abdul Malik, Old Kent Road Mosque

Figure 5: The *mihrab*, *minbar* and *qibla* wall of the main men's prayer hall

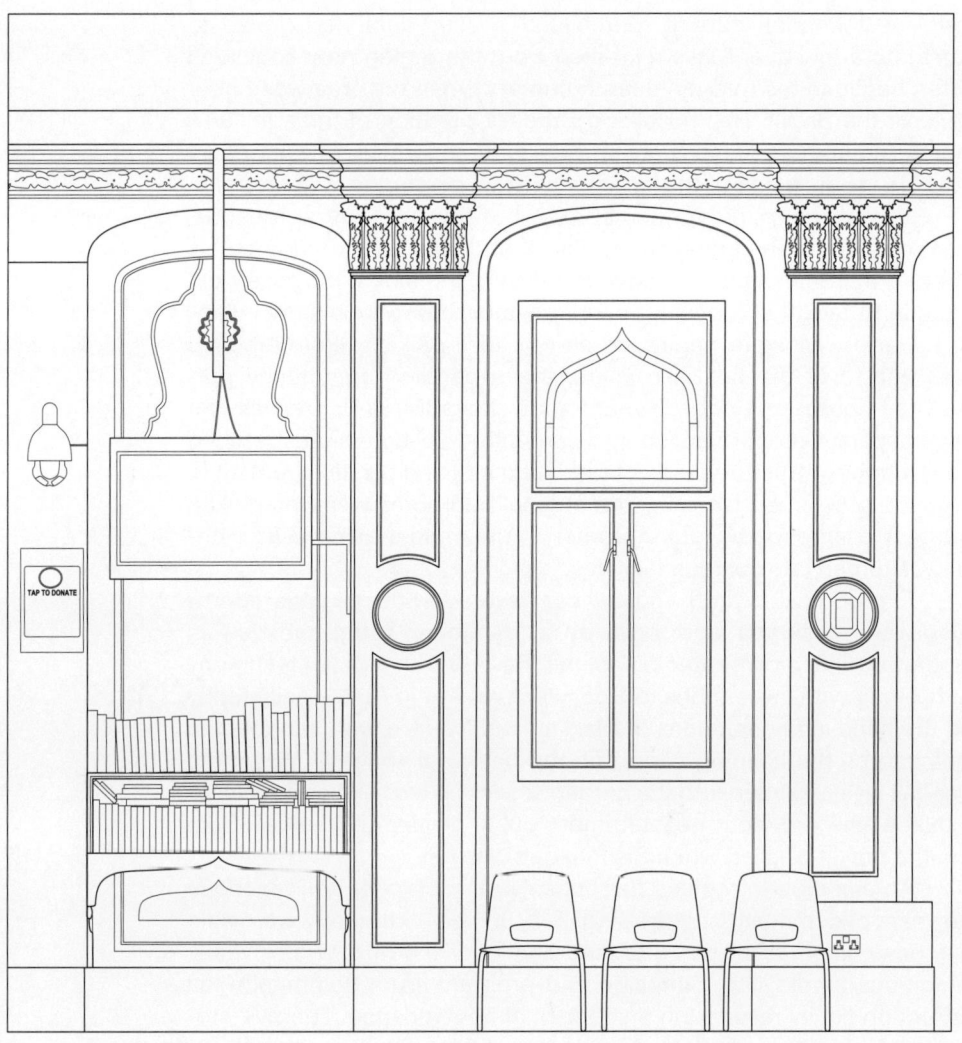

Figure 6: The features of a wall in the main men's prayer hall

Case Study 3: Harrow Central Mosque

The converted house was a prevalent typology for mosques throughout the twentieth century, in part because it offered a modest space that was easily adapted and already fitted with washing facilities. Although communities often outgrow the house-mosque, even today one-third of mosques in Britain are former homes.

In 1984, a predominantly Pakistani Muslim community in Harrow, a north-west London suburb, purchased a semi-detached house to convert into a mosque. Mass migration from the region now known as Pakistan began in the mid-nineteenth century when the area was under the rule of the British Raj. Following Britain's partition of India in 1947, an increasing number of Pakistani families settled permanently in Britain, and the UK is now home to the largest Pakistani community in Europe.

One of the founding members of the Harrow Central Mosque, Mohammed Abdullah Quereshi, recalled that it was a visit made by his children to the Shah Jahan Mosque in Woking, the oldest purpose-built mosque in Britain, that motivated him to establish one for his own community. Harrow Mosque began life as one of a pair of semi-detached houses and, over the next ten years, the expanding community purchased the house next door. The entrance doors (Figure 7), originally for the two separate properties, led into one united space which stretched into a temporary structure made of modest metal and plastic sheeting to enlarge the prayer hall. Upstairs, the original bedrooms were interlinked to create two large rooms for the women to pray, and the domestic bathroom was turned into ablution facilities.

The original *mihrab* and *minbar*, layered with religious adornments, were designed and built by a member of the mosque in collaboration with a carpenter in Kashmir (Figure 8). The Muslim testimony of faith, along with invocations to God, were written in Arabic calligraphy along the band, and depictions of Makkah and Medina were mounted in frames and on the hanging carpet on the back wall (Figure 9). When the prayer hall was extended into the garden, a second less elaborate *mihrab* was built at the new south-easternmost point, closest to Makkah, from where the prayer was led when the mosque was full.

An ambition to replace the house with a purpose-built mosque led to years of community fundraising. In 1999, the community were able to purchase an adjacent piece of land and, over the next twelve years, an ambitious fundraising campaign and programme of community-led construction finally resulted in a substantial new mosque. The five-storey structure has been built in the Ottoman style with a shallow dome and needle minaret. A *mihrab* made from inscribed marble imported from Turkey completes the prayer hall. Fundraising continues for a calligraphic frieze around the building.

As the earlier house-mosque no longer serves as a place of prayer, it has partially returned to domestic use. With the external signage and interior details removed, the building's historic function as a mosque is forgotten; the temporary extension has been pulled down, and the former prayer space lies empty as the building awaits residential redevelopment. The early iteration of the Harrow Mosque, created through a series of adaptations, now only survives in photographs and oral testimony. Through 3D scans and interviews, a record has been formed of its role in this formative stage of British mosque communities. As an unlisted site, the structure could be demolished at any time.

> We spent about twenty years in the house-mosque while we were collecting money to build a new masjid. Once we had the donations, we started construction, which took about five to seven years. I remember it was 7 December 2011, the first time that we prayed here in the morning. And we were all quite happy to move here because it's big – in fact, it's a huge space. We slowly started to organise events as well: apart from private parties, we do special classes, madrasah classes, English classes, maths classes, Islamic classes. The number of people increased day by day. As soon as people knew there were big events, there were opportunities to provide other services as well. People know they can come forward and join us, which is very good. We have a lot of people here, especially during Friday prayers.

Raja Ali, Harrow Central Mosque

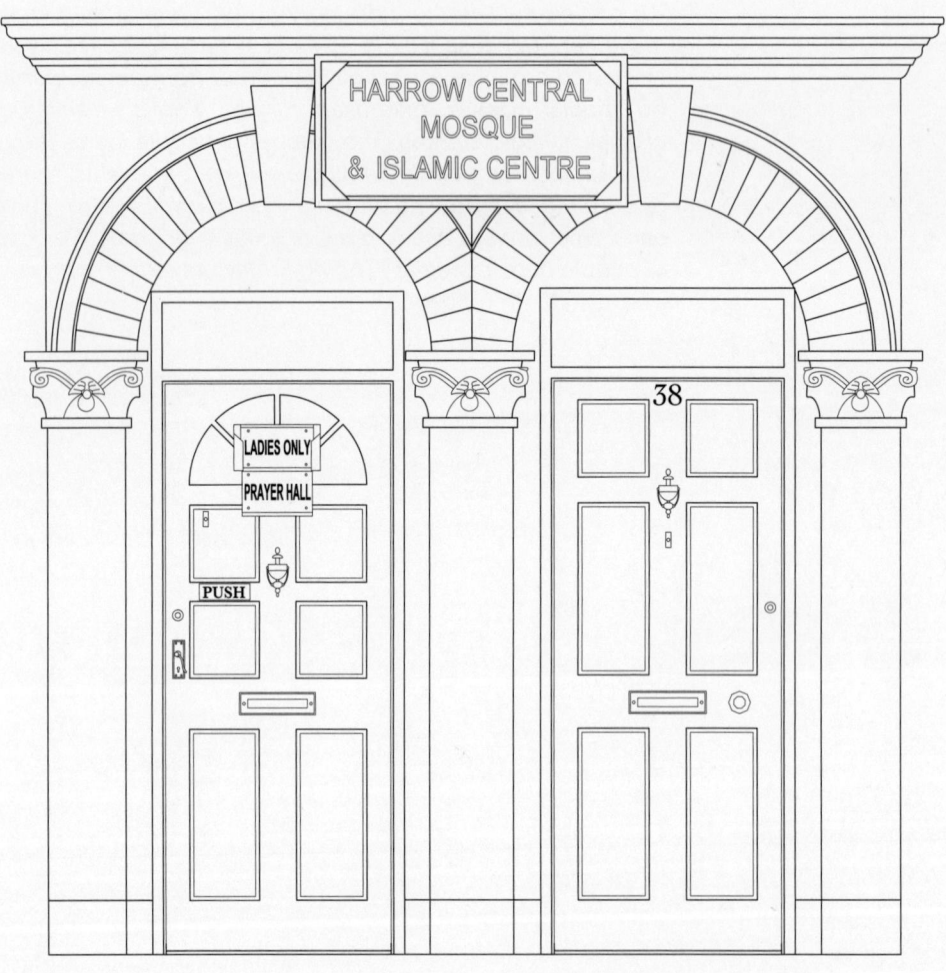

Figure 7: Entrance doors to the pair of houses

Figure 8: The *mihrab* in the main prayer room of the house-mosque

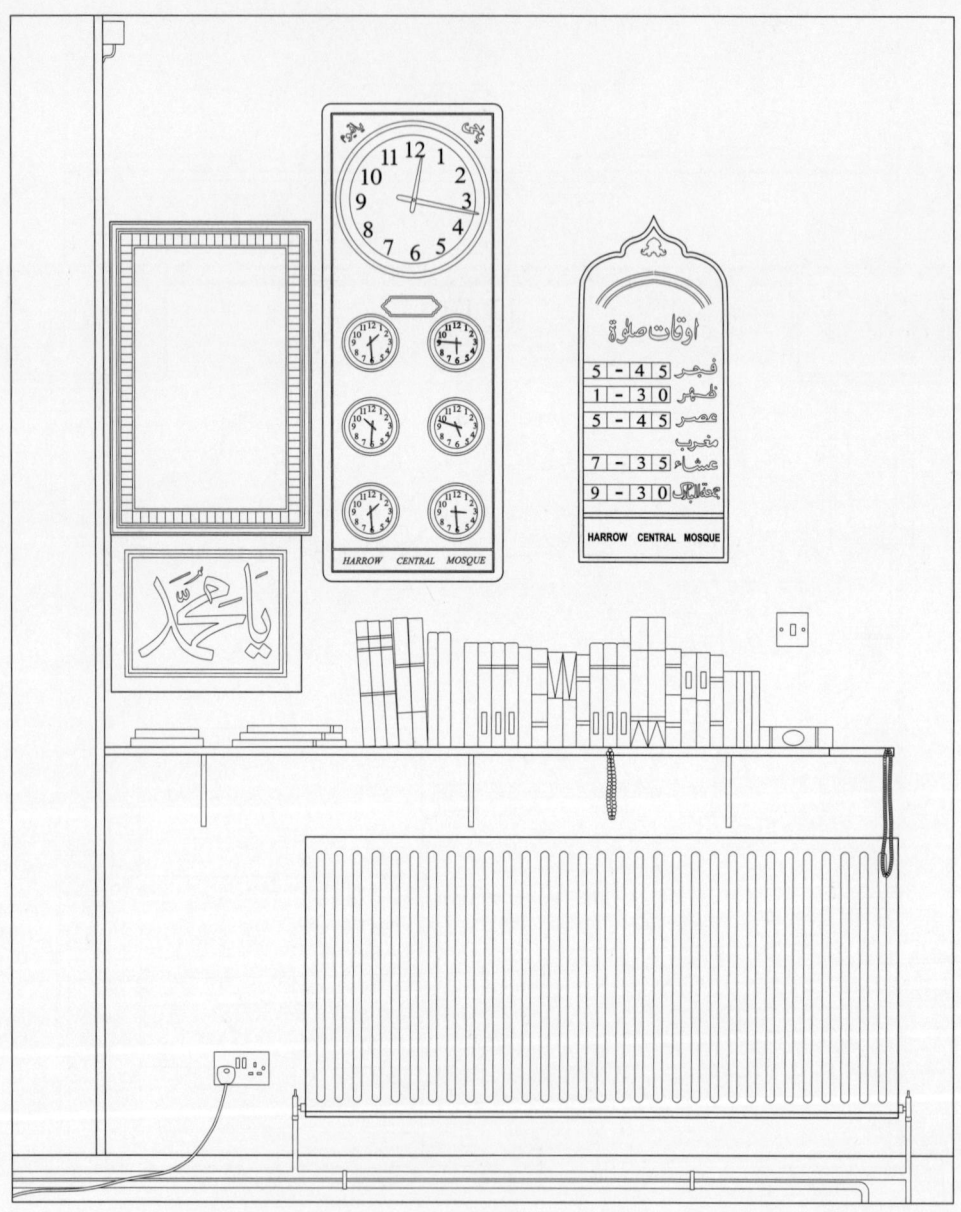

Figure 9: The *qibla* wall in the main prayer room of the house-mosque

3D digital Lidar scan of the Brick Lane Mosque, showing the lower and upper men's prayer halls, the classrooms in the roofspace, and the women's prayer room in the rear part of the basement vault

3D digital Lidar scan of the Old Kent Road Mosque showing the men's prayer hall on the first floor and women's on the ground floor, with additional worship and teaching spaces alongside

3D digital Lidar scan of the Harrow Central Mosque and Masood Islamic Centre, showing the original house mosque alongside its purpose-built replacement

Assembly: performing the materiality of Muslim prayer space

Julie Marsh

Congregation in conversation at *Assembly* site-performance

Assembly: performing the materiality of Muslim prayer space
Julie Marsh

At the heart of every mosque lies its community. As each congregation expands the mosque adapts and transforms to meet its needs. The building, in turn, informs the way in which the community develops within the architecture of the site. The congregation and building evolve together, producing a symbiotic relationship unique to each Muslim community. The *Three British Mosques* exhibition for the 2021 Venice Biennale highlights the significance of this relationship through a social archive of each mosque featured in the exhibition. Films of congregational prayer show the community in action, and individual worshippers tell personal stories of their relationship to their mosque in a series of interviews.

This cinematic archive has its roots in research conducted for *Assembly*, a site-specific visual research project made and exhibited in Brick Lane Mosque, Old Kent Road Mosque and Harrow Mosque in London from 2018 to 2021. Made in collaboration with each mosque community, *Assembly* attempts to re-enact a performance of congregational prayer via 1:1 floor projections. An automated motorised camera is used to record the Jumu'ah (Friday) prayer from above; this film is then projected back on to the carpet on which the prayer was performed using a lens mounted on the same overhead track from which it was filmed. This projection – a record and a trace of worship – provides an opportunity for others to experience prayer *in situ*, via the artwork. At the end of each residency, the mosque community invites the general public into their prayer spaces to experience the Jumu'ah prayer via the site-specific performances.

Assembly uses this artist's methodology of 'site-integrity' which employs artistic devices to perform the social, religious, architectural and institutional practices that take place in a religious site. A mosque community is not a fixed entity, but is continually in the process of being made by the everyday practice of Islam. When sites of worship are reduced to representations, the performative and experiential qualities are lost. 'Site-integrity' repositions the act of representation from its retrospective or projective dimensions towards that which is experiential. Therefore, *Assembly* should not be regarded as a representation of a space, and still less one of individual worshippers, but rather as an attempt to perform the mosque as it actually exists. Both the buildings and the communities it forms are re-enacted each time the piece is performed, in a relational process between the site, worshippers, artwork and audience.

Assembly directly responds to the religious and social practices operating in each mosque. At the start of each residency the mosque committee discuss what is and isn't permissible, providing clear guidelines to follow when making the artwork. In all three mosques the filming process needs to be non-intrusive; the camera not permitted to film in front of people praying nor can it show their faces, therefore the worshipers are filmed discreetly from above. Each congregation become fully involved in the artwork's development with male members of the congregation involved practically in the production, especially during the Friday

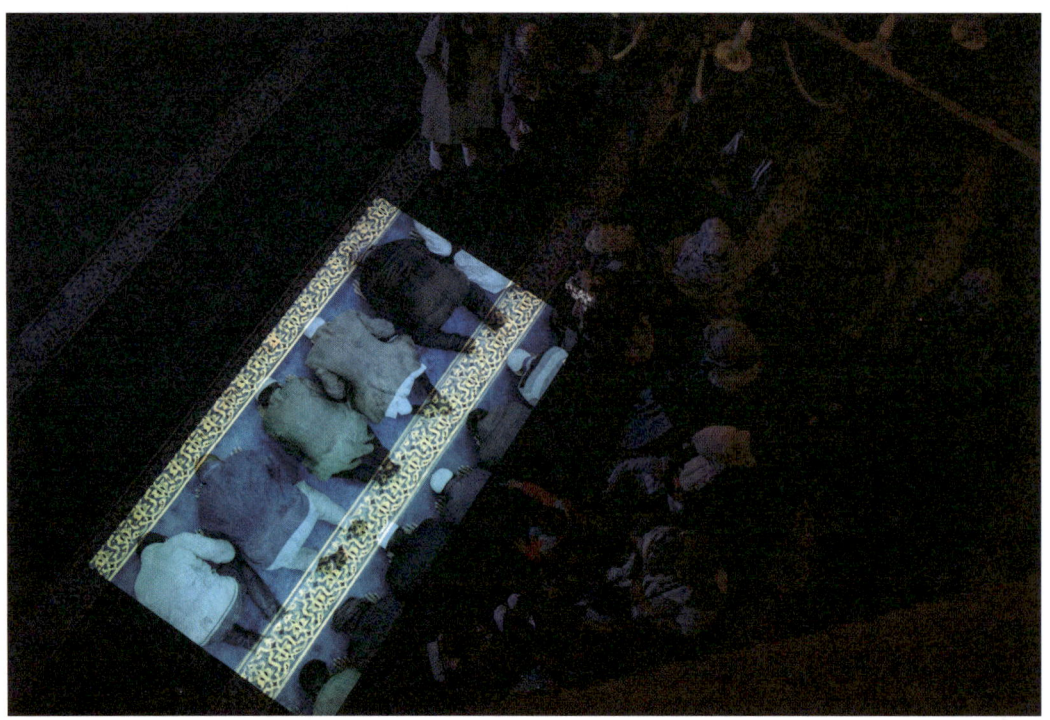

Moving floor projection in main prayer hall

Site-performance for local schools

Jumu'ah prayer, when the artist is not allowed to access to the main prayer hall. This involvement builds a level of trust within the community and ownership of the artwork as they start to refer to the work as 'our' film:

> It is something that I've been involved in over the last month or two, I always help set up the rig at the start of prayer and take it down once the filming is complete. I think our film is really effective, it makes you think of unison, everyone in the world at this time is praying towards one direction who is a Muslim. (Congregation member)

Assembly allows each mosque to fulfil their mission 'to work closely with the wider community, members of different faith and non-faith' by opening up the artwork and site to a public audience. *Assembly* dissolves the perception that the mosque is a 'no-go area' outside of the Muslim community, providing an opportunity for non-Muslims to understand the religious practices taking place, without feeling like a voyeur:

> I was always curious to see and know what was taking place, but it was obviously a strict no-go area. Having the opportunity to witness prayer through Assembly, and not feel as though I was intruding was really incredible. I found it a rare, meditative and moving experience. (Audience feedback)

The artwork becomes a point of reflection for a deeper understanding of Islamic faith, challenging social perceptions that might unconsciously exist. The importance of establishing relationships within the younger generation is also evident during local school visits where primary school children, staff and parents visit the artwork. The madrasah pupils gain a sense of belonging and pride as they show the visiting children 'their mosque' while the local school children learn about Islamic faith and culture through play and interaction.

Assembly also provides an opportunity for each congregation to consider and reflect upon their own religious practices. The projection provides a point of contemplation to explore thoughts in relation to worship, time, space and being. The worshippers experience 'themselves' in the *active* sense as they interact with their own image performing ritual prayer:

> The projection opened my eyes to the physical act of prayer. Of movement and repetition. Because my view or senses are often fixed on a focal point (the imam), I didn't really consider my own movements until seeing the image of myself in prayer. (Congregation feedback)

Each site performance allows access for men and women to both male and female spaces of worship, temporarily dissolving the gender segregation within the mosque. This provides an opportunity for the congregation to also reflect upon the social structures present in site and share views and opinions within their own community. These conversations, personal histories and projected futures form insights into the individuals and the community they form part of. The *Three British Mosques* exhibition provides an opportunity to record these communities at differing stages in their development, discovering and preserving the history and heritage of each congregation and its place of prayer.

Filming at Brick Lane Mosque

Film still: Brick Lane Mosque women's prayer room

Film still: Old Kent Road Mosque women's prayer hall

Film still: Brick Lane Mosque main prayer hall

Film still: Old Kent Road Mosque main prayer hall

Film still: Harrow Mosque main prayer hall

Acknowledgements

The editors would like to thank everyone who contributed to the research, writing and production of this book. This project would not have been possible without support from the mosque communities of Brick Lane Jamme Masjid, Old Kent Road Mosque & Islamic Cultural Centre, and Harrow Central Mosque & Masood Islamic Centre. We are particularly grateful to the following people who agreed to be interviewed for the project: Abdal Ullah, Al-haj Yousuf Kamaly, Naima Ahmed, Raja Ali, Ahmed Akhoundzadeh, Mohammed Abdullah Quereshi, Razia Rabbani, Kamal Louani, Sideequah Dawodu, Saidat Oketunde, Abdul Malik, Abdul Lateef Yusuf, Imam Kazeem Fatai and Rashidat Hussain. Thank you to Anusheh Zia for facilitating interviews at Harrow Central Mosque.

The Ramadan Pavilion is being created in collaboration with the Ramadan Tent Project, the University of Westminster and AKT II. The Pavilion of Applied Arts at the 17th International Architecture Exhibition – La Biennale di Venezia has been made possible thanks to the lead supporter Volkswagen Group and donors to the Venice Biennale Architecture Fund in memory of Dr Martin Roth, former director of the Victoria and Albert Museum. The exhibition fabrication is the work of Michael Short of Remshore Creations; and graphics are by Boris Meister of V&A Design, with thanks to Irfan Ahmed of One Agency. The films, stills of which are reproduced in this book, were made by Julie Marsh, with Jonny Fuller-Rowell as cinematographer and Johnny Titheridge as sound recordist. The production of the films was made possible thanks to funding from CREAM (Centre for Research and Education in Arts and Media) and the PILOT (Practical and Innovative Live Outcomes Testing) research funding scheme at the University of Westminster. Technical drawings of each mosque element, reproduced between pages 88-100, are the work of Leen Ajlan. Digital 3D scans of each mosque, reproduced on pages 102-107, were made by Guy Sinclair from the Fabrication Lab at the University of Westminster. David Gallagher and Tom Berndorfer, DGA Architects, have generously loaned steel test pieces for the Brick Lane minaret for display in Venice. Finally, a special thank you to the Biennale project managers, Alexandra Willett and Catriona Macdonald.

The authors would like to thank curators at the V&A who have offered guidance on the project and the content of the book. Many thanks are due to Olivia Horsfall Turner, Omniya Abdel Barr, Mariam Rosser-Owen, Nick Barnard and Navjot Mangat. Thanks also to Rebekah Coffman and Matthew Wells. Lastly, many thanks to Nick Jones for editing, and to Daniel Fletcher and Foolscap Editions who have supported the V&A and University of Westminster in the creative direction and production of this publication. This book has been generously funded by Gregory Sporton, Head of School, Westminster School of Arts, and the Victoria and Albert Museum.

The Centre for Research in Education, Arts and Media at the University of Westminster is proud to support and sponsor this important project. Julie Marsh and Shahed Saleem from the university, working with Christopher Turner and Ella Kilgallon from the Victoria and Albert Museum, have completed an impressive body of work over the past three years that responds to the 2021 Venice Architecture Biennale's theme, *How will we live together?*. The message from this project, and particularly the enthusiastic participation of the community, is inescapable: we need each other.

The encounter between Marsh and Saleem's approaches sheds light on the experiences of their subjects. At the heart of Marsh's work – and she picks up on this in her essay (page 109) – is the idea of ephemeral light and projection as a mode of contemplation. Her site-specific pieces are able to be both real and unreal at once. They capture the beauty of aspiration and inspiration, both words of breath and soul quite central to the act of worship and, indeed, of being. For his part, Saleem points us to the virtual as the adaptation of an idea that is forever being reinvented for its context, the necessity to give form to need. The interchangeability of significance between site and person shows how closely these things are intertwined.

Marsh and Saleem's work displays the commitment we have as a research group and a university to contribute to the reality around us, to situate ourselves within our communities. We are grateful for the partnership we have had with the V&A, and hope this publication will give further life to an outstanding project, while illustrating for readers the subtle weave of community with art and the spirit.

Gregory Sporton, Head of School, Westminster School of Arts

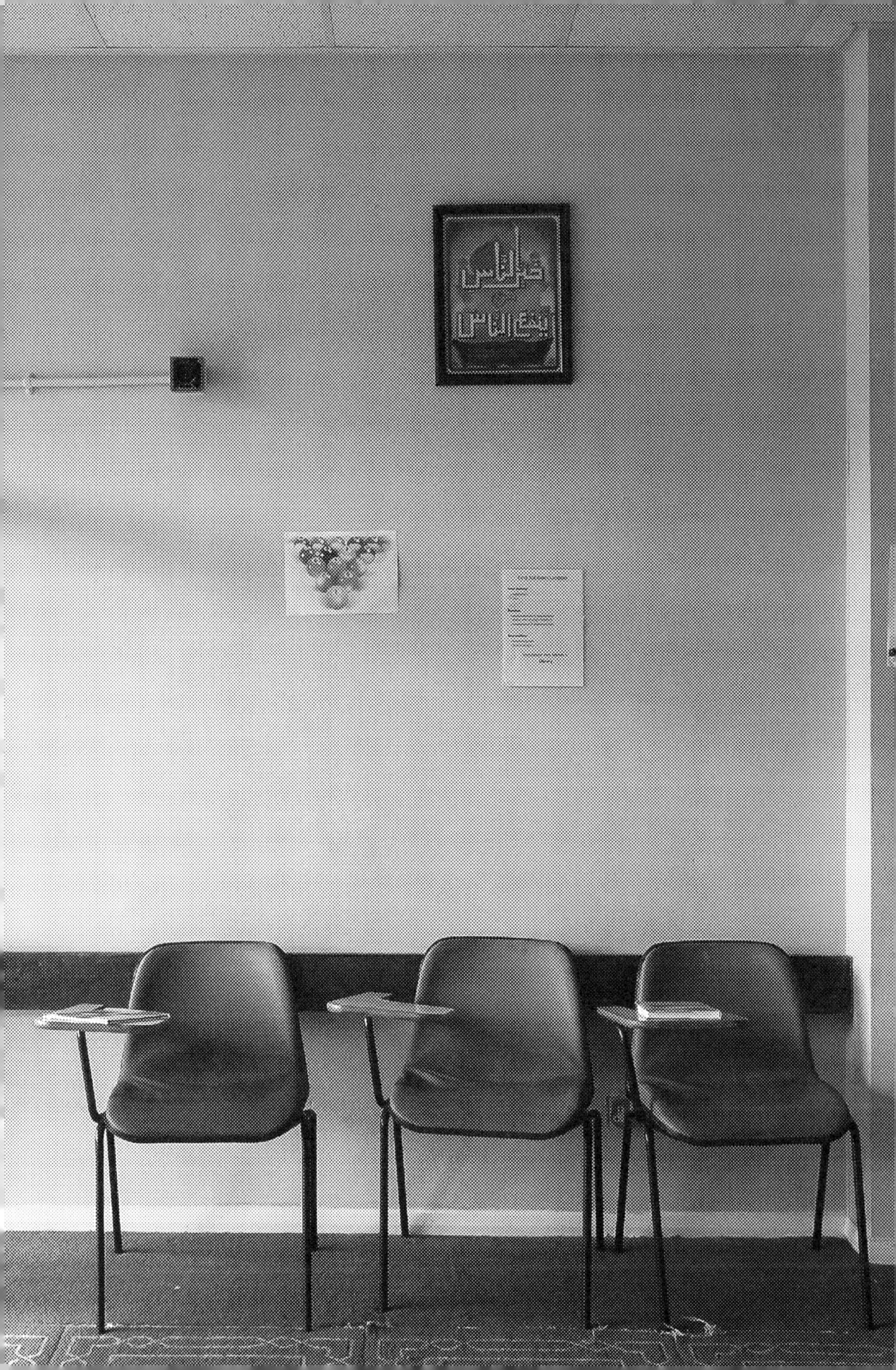

Biographies

Christopher Turner is the Keeper of Design, Architecture and Digital at the Victoria and Albert Museum. He is co-curator of the exhibition *Three British Mosques* at La Biennale di Venezia 2021, and of the Ramadan Pavilion, an installation planned for the London Festival of Architecture 2022.

Shahed Saleem is a practising architect and design studio leader at the University of Westminster School of Architecture. He is author of the book *The British Mosque: An Architectural and Social History* (Historic England, 2018). Saleem is co-curator of *Three British Mosques* and is the architect of the Ramadan Pavilion.

Julie Marsh is Senior Lecturer and Researcher at the Centre for Research and Education in Arts and Media at the University of Westminster. She is an artist and filmmaker and the creator of *Assembly*, a series of site performance films made in collaboration with London mosque communities.

Ella Kilgallon is Assistant Curator, Designs at the Victoria and Albert Museum. She is co-curator of *Three British Mosques* and the Ramadan Pavilion.

Published on the occasion of the 17th International Architecture Exhibition – La Biennale di Venezia 2021.

Three British Mosques, Pavilion of Applied Arts, Special Project between the V&A and La Biennale di Venezia, 22 May to 21 November 2021.

© 2021 V&A, London; Foolscap Editions, London; Shahed Saleem and the authors. All visual material included in this publication © Shahed Saleem, Julie Marsh, V&A unless otherwise stated.

All rights reserved. No part of this publication may be reproduced, stored in a retrieval system or transmitted in any form or by any means, electronic, mechanical, photocopying, recording or otherwise without prior permission of both V&A and Foolscap Editions.

Edited by Shahed Saleem, Christopher Turner, Ella Kilgallon
Sub-edited by Nick Jones
Creative Direction and Production by Daniel Fletcher
Design by William Lyall
Printing by Kopa

Cover image: adaptation of drawings from Shahed Saleem's sketchbooks in the V&A's collection, museum nos. E.1048 to 1049-2019.

Select bibliography:
Full reference from p. 57, Oludamini Ogunnaike, 'The *Mihrab*: Reflections on Form, Function and Symbolism', in *The Art of Orientation: An Exploration of the Mosque Through Objects* (Hirmer Verlag, 2021), pp. 201-217.

Rodney Searight and Jennifer M. Scarce, *A Middle Eastern Journey: artists on their travels from the collection of Rodney Searight* (Talbot Rice Art Centre, 1980).

Tim Stanley (ed.), with Mariam Rosser-Owen and Stephen Vernoit, *Palace and Mosque: Islamic Art from the Middle East* (V&A Publications, 2004).

First published by V&A, London and Foolscap Editions, London 2021.

ISBN: 978-1-9997990-6-9

Foolscap Editions is an independent publisher founded in 2016 that works in close collaboration with artists and institutions to release books and special editions.

foolscap-editions.com
info@foolscap-editions.com